$\mathscr{P}$ENNSYLVANIA
impressions

FARCOUNTRY
PRESS

photography by
John McGrail

Right: Cross-country skiers take to the trail along Wissahickon Creek in 8,700-acre Fairmount Park in northwestern Philadelphia.

Title page: Visitors who climb the stone tower atop Bowman's Hill are rewarded with this view of Washington Crossing Historic Park and the Delaware River. The park honors George Washington and the American soldiers who crossed the icy Delaware on Christmas Night, 1776, for a surprise—and victorious—attack on Trenton, New Jersey.

Front cover: The Isaac Potts House served as George Washington's headquarters at Valley Forge during the Revolutionary War.

Back cover: One of the oldest and largest arboreta in the northeast, Tyler Arboretum features 650 acres of rare plants, ancient trees, hiking trails, and historic structures.

Below: The decorative use of hex signs is a tradition brought to America by the Pennsylvania Dutch.

ISBN 13: 978-1-56037-342-1
ISBN 10: 1-56037-342-3
Photography © 2005 John McGrail, all rights reserved
© 2005 Farcountry Press

Created, produced, and designed in the United States.
Printed in China.

09   08   07   06   05   1   2   3   4   5

Above: Re-enactors fire flintlock rifles at Brandywine Battlefield Park, Chadds Ford. On September 11, 1777, George Washington and young French General Lafayette commanded American troops against the British here on Brandywine Creek. Although the American Continental Army lost, it slowed the British advance.

Facing page: At the Drake Well Museum, Titusville, exhibits tell the story of this, the world's first commercially successful oil well, built by Edwin Drake in 1859.

Above: A Stearman and a Travelair Speedwing enjoy the sky above Bucks County near Erwinna.

Facing page: These cheerful tulips are among 11,000 different types of plants on Longwood Gardens' 1,050 acres at Kennett Square.

Facing page: All aboard! Visitors to the Railroad Museum of Pennsylvania in Strasburg can explore more than a hundred historic locomotives and railcars.

Right: In its huge hangar at Reading, the Mid-Atlantic Air Museum exhibits airplanes of all sizes and eras, from biplanes to helicopters, bombers to classic airliners.

Below: This coal wagon once dumped fuel into basement coal bins. It now sits in the Pennsylvania Anthracite Heritage Museum in Scranton, amid exhibits on the social and working lives of coal-region residents.

Following pages: Prosperous farms fill Luzerne County's Conyngham Valley.

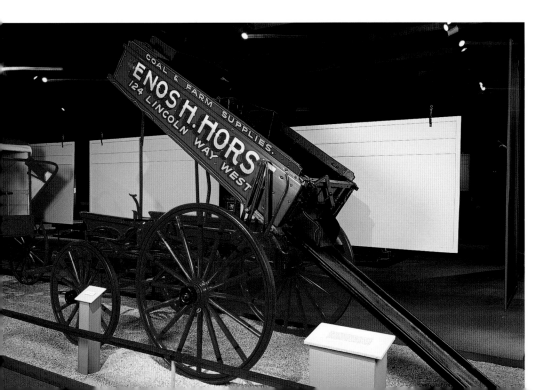

Above: Ephrata Cloister Historic Site, at the town of Ephrata, features buildings that once housed a communal, celibate religious colony created by Conrad Beissel of Germany in 1732.

Facing page: Hopewell Furnace, a restored industrial village, is now a National Historic Site near Birdsboro. From 1771 to 1883, it bustled with iron making and fabricating.

Facing page: White-tailed deer, the most numerous game animal in North America, are all around Pennsylvania.

Left: Flying high on a snowboard is one way to enjoy the twenty slopes at Scranton's Montage Mountain Ski Resort, a year-round family resort.

Below: Punxsutawney Phil and his handlers from the Punxsutawney Groundhog Club let the nation know whether to expect six more weeks of winter after each February 2. If he sees his shadow as dawn touches Gobbler's Knob—watch out for snowflakes!

Following pages: Here in the Assembly Chamber of Independence Hall, Philadelphia, during the hot summer of 1787, delegates from the thirteen states wrote their new nation's constitution. Eleven years earlier, Thomas Jefferson, John Adams, Benjamin Franklin, Robert R. Livingston, and Roger Sherman drafted the Declaration of Independence in this room.

Left: Its core built in 1700 and its current English Gothic appearance achieved from 1850 to 1863, Historic Grange Estate at Havertown is open for tours of the mansion, summer kitchen, and carriage house.

Facing page: Tyler Arboretum, Media, is spread across more than 650 acres that include ancient and rare trees, historic buildings, and hiking trails.

Above: Amish buggies travel at brisk trots throughout Lancaster County, the heart of Pennsylvania Dutch country.

Left: Tobacco cures in an Amish barn, Lancaster County.

Above: The Pennsylvania Dutch brought America the European tradition of decorating with mystical, symbolic hex signs, like these near Hamburg.

Facing page: From 1913 to 1916, Henry C. Mercer built the Mercer Museum's six-story concrete tower, where he collected folk art, tools, furnishings, and non-mechanized vehicles. Today the Mercer Museum in Doylestown is a National Historic Landmark, and this view of the Central Court reveals a codfish dory and a whaleboat.

Left: The National Shrine of Our Lady of Czestochowa at Doylestown is a Polish Catholic spiritual and pilgrimage center. A statue of Pope John Paul II stands in front of the Shrine.

Facing page: Dedicated by President Theodore Roosevelt in 1906, the Pennsylvania State Capitol in Harrisburg displays Italian Renaissance design, with its dome modeled upon that of St. Peter's Basilica in Rome.

Below: Andalusia, a Greek Revival mansion begun in 1797 by Nicholas Biddle near the town of Andalusia, has been home to his descendents for more than 150 years.

Above: Fly fishing is a pleasure along parts of the 128-mile-long Schuylkill River, the "Revolutionary River" that passes Valley Forge and flows through Philadelphia.

Facing page: Among the twenty-two named waterfalls in lushly forested Ricketts Glen State Park, the highest—Ganoga Falls, seen here—drops ninety-four feet.

Left: A screech owls stands on high alert.

Facing page: Two hundred thirty-two miles of the 2,155-mile Appalachian Trail wander diagonally across Pennsylvania, offering vistas such as this one.

Below: Near Kempton, Hawk Mountain Sanctuary is a raptor watcher's paradise, as thousands of hawks, eagles, and falcons navigate among its ridgetops.

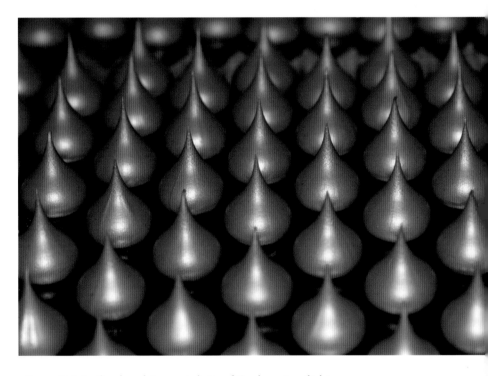

Above and left: In the chocolate-scented city of Hershey, streetlights are shaped like the chocolate maker's Hershey Kisses, in production above.

Facing page: Wildwater Kingdom at Allentown offers the perfect spot for hot summer afternoons.

Above: Glessner Bridge near Shanksville has offered weather protection for those crossing Stonycreek River since 1881.

Facing page: In Somerset County, an elaborate hex star represents good luck for this barn and its users.

Following pages: Modern Pittsburgh is a far cry from the seventeenth-century fur post and successive British and French army forts that were the first buildings here at the head of the Ohio River.

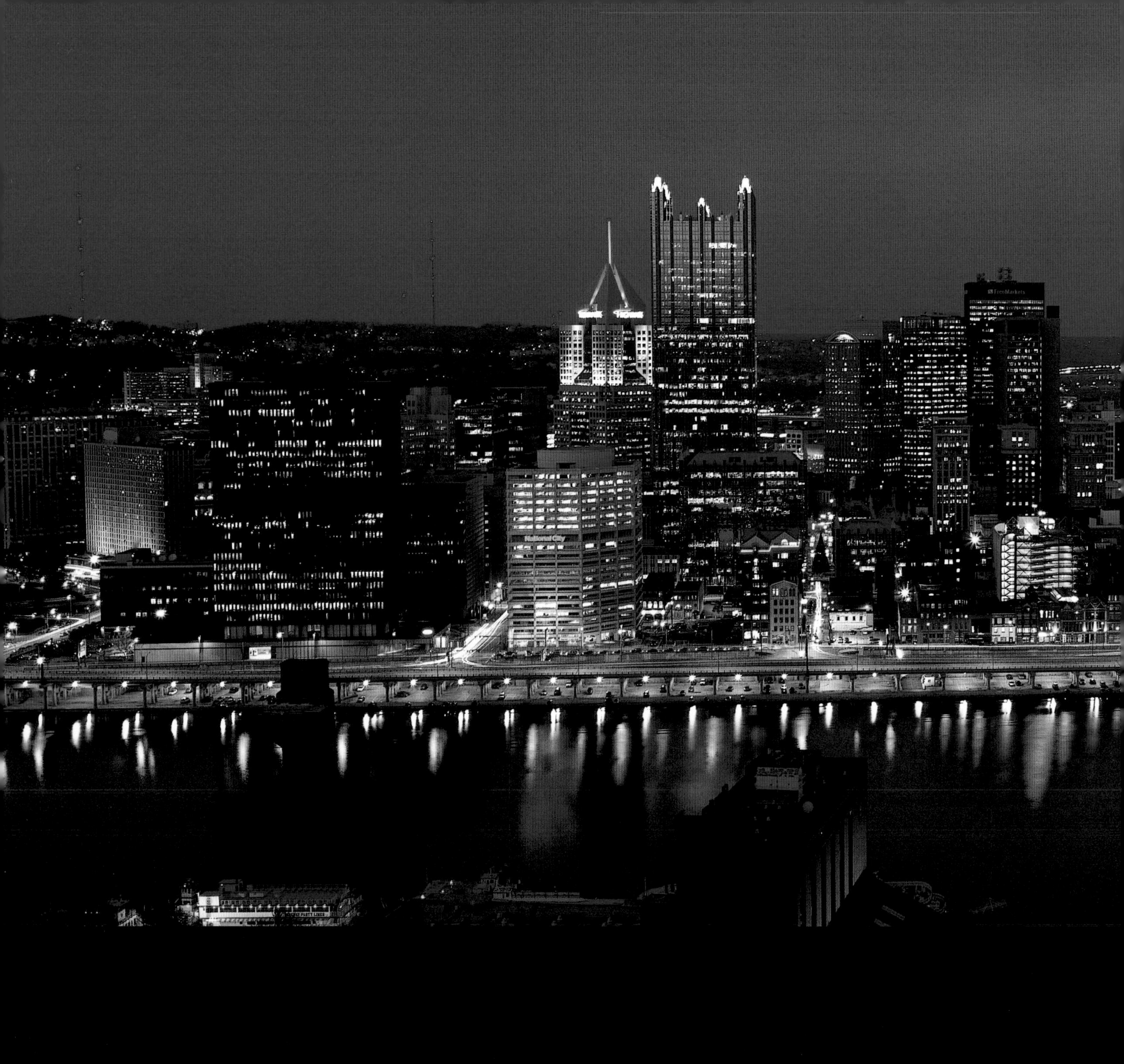
National City
FreeMarkets

Above: Daniel Boone began his westering life in 1734, here at the Daniel Boone Homestead, Birdsboro. The modern museum tells the story of self-sufficient pioneer life in America.

Facing page: In December 1776, the Thompson-Neely House in Washington Crossing Historic Park was the headquarters for William Alexander, the British earl who became a Continental Army general. He and his troops were assigned to prevent British forces from crossing the Delaware River into Pennsylvania.

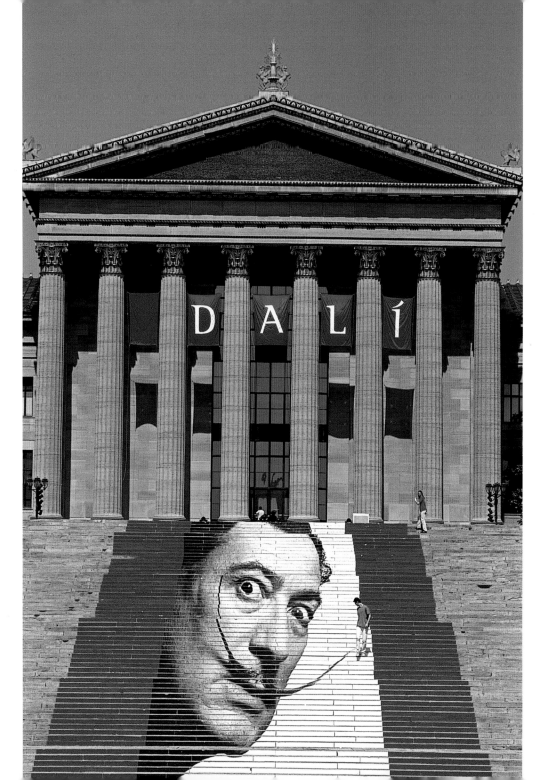

Left: As the only American venue for a Salvador Dalí (1904–1989) retrospective on his birth centennial, the Philadelphia Museum of Art created this appropriate portrait of the flamboyant Surrealist painter.

Facing page: Rowers press their shell along the Schuylkill River past the Philadelphia Museum of Art (background) and Fairmount waterworks.

Above: Asa Packer—railroad magnate, philanthropist, and Lehigh University founder—commissioned this 11,000-square-foot Italianate mansion in 1861 in Mauch Chunk (an Indian phrase meaning "Bear Mountain"). In 1953, when Olympic gold medalist Jim Thorpe was buried in the town, Mauch Chunk renamed itself Jim Thorpe.

Facing page: Located outside Shanksville until a permanent memorial is completed, this temporary one honors the passengers of United Airlines Flight 93, who fought back when terrorists hijacked their plane on September 11, 2001. Benches with passengers' names face where Flight 93 crashed, several hundred yards from here, during their fight for control of the aircraft.

Above: Preserved homes, stores, and churches of Eckley Miners' Village in Weatherly reveal life in one of the first company-owned coal mining communities, which was founded in 1854.

Right: Jutting into Lake Erie at the city of Erie, Presque Isle State Park offers Pennsylvania's only surf beach, along with cross-country skiing in winter.

Above: On forty acres of a former Scranton rail yard, Steamtown National Historic Site exhibits railroad history from 1850 through 1950, including three operating locomotives.

Right: Near Scranton, visitors can tour the Lackawanna Coal Mine, visit with a miner, and view three levels of the former hard-coal mine.

Facing page: A statue of the Marquis de Lafayette, the French general who aided the American and French revolutions, overlooks Lafayette College in Easton. When the town's citizens founded the college in 1826, they named it in his honor.

45

Above: The intriguing Pagoda, a seven-story resort built in 1907 atop Mount Penn in Reading, is now open to tourists and houses an art gallery and the Berks Arts Council.

Right: Allentown's Dorney Park lights the night with a hundred colorful rides.

Following pages: Tuscarora Mountain's long ridge, part of the Appalachian chain, is broken only by a tunnel for the Pennsylvania Turnpike.

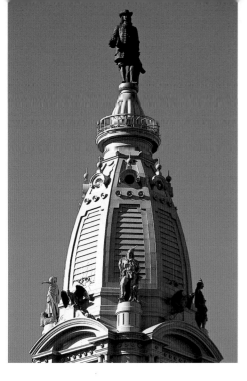

Above: The thirty-six-foot statue of Pennsylvania-founder William Penn atop Philadelphia City Hall, created by Alexander Milne Calder and placed in 1894, is known familiarly as "Billy Penn."

Right: Swann Memorial Fountain in Philadelphia's Logan Circle includes three large sculptures representing the Delaware and Schuylkill rivers and Wissahickon Creek. Installed in 1924, the work was designed by Alexander Stirling Calder, son of the "Billy Penn" sculptor.

Facing page: The flags along Benjamin Franklin Parkway offer a colorful salute from Pennsylvania to the nations of the world.

Above: In the Pocono Mountains, Bushkill Falls' series of eight waterfalls form the "Niagara of Pennsylvania" and include 100-foot Main Falls.

Right: The Edgar Kaufmann family of Pittsburgh commissioned Frank Lloyd Wright, in 1934, to design their weekend retreat of Fallingwater at their favorite spot along Bear Run near Ohiopyle. He chose to place the building over the Bear Run waterfall.

Above: Lake Ontelaunee, a reservoir for the city of Reading, is a site for good fishing, hiking, and picnicking.

Left: Fireworks paint the summer night outside the Philadelphia Museum of Art, silhouetting *The Lion Fighter*, a statue by Albert Wolff (1814–1892).

Above: Re-enactors march at Brandywine Battlefield Park, Chadds Ford.

Right: The Boulder Field in Hickory Run State Park, near White Haven, reveals past glaciation of Pennsylvania and is a National Natural Landmark. Melting glaciers dropped these rocks as the Earth warmed.

Above: Firemarks, like this one in Philadelphia, indicated the private fire company to which a colonial American household subscribed.

Right: Inside the Pennsylvania State Capitol, the grand staircase rises to the commonwealth's house and senate chambers.

Below: Works of stained glass art in Fireman's Hall portray firefighters in action. Operated by the Philadelphia Fire Department, the museum covers American firefighting from 1731 to the present, and is housed in a historic fire hall.

Above: This beautiful vase is an example of the "Honesdale glass" designed by Christian Dorflinger (1828–1915) and created at his White Mills factory, which now houses the Dorflinger Glass Museum.

Right: The late eighteenth century for average American farm families comes back to life at Colonial Pennsylvania Plantation in Ridley Creek State Park, Media.

Facing page: The homey back entrances to President James Buchanan's mansion, Wheatland, in Lancaster—a house that is wide but only two rooms deep. Buchanan was the nation's only bachelor president, and also the only president from Pennsylvania.

Above: Tyler State Park, Bucks County, dons winter garb.

Right: In Ricketts Glen State Park, Jack Frost applies his icy hand to one of the many waterfalls.

Facing page: Grandview Cemetery, Johnstown, includes 777 graves of unidentified victims of the 1889 Johnstown Flood, when a burst dam killed 2,209 people within a ten-minute period.

Above: A pair of Amish girls walk the quiet roads near their home.

Below and right: Tidy Amish farms, operated on literal horsepower, fill Lancaster County.

Above: Restored railroad cabooses are the sleeping rooms in Strasburg's unique Red Caboose Motel, where a Victorian dining car serves as the restaurant.

Right: Crayons in the making at the Crayola factory, Easton, which offers tours and hands-on activities for all ages.

Far right: Guided whitewater raft trips thrill many Pocono Mountains visitors.

Following pages: Valley Forge National Historic Park, near Plymouth Meeting, was where George Washington and 11,000 starving and ill-clad American troops camped from December 1777 to mid-June 1778.

Above: Tourists explore rural Bucks County, observing one of the covered bridges from their hot-air balloon.

Left: At Mill Bridge Village near Paradise, exhibits and interpreters describe Amish life in the 1700s.

Above: America's oldest brewery, Pottsville's Yuengling Brewery has been family owned and operated since 1829, and continues to produce boutique beers.

Right: France's patron saint, Joan of Arc, created in bronze by French sculptor Emmanuel Fremiet (1824–1910) and later gilded, is located just east of the Philadelphia Museum of Art.

Facing page: Formerly a downtown Scranton railroad depot, the Radisson Lackawanna Station Hotel has placed its lobby below the depot's vaulted Tiffany glass skylight.

Above: From 1832 to 1931, the Delaware Canal's sixty miles paralleled the Delaware River, carrying freight and passengers until 1866, and after that, only coal. Today's visitors find the near-silence of canal-boat travel in the Delaware & Lehigh National Heritage Corridor simply amazing.

Left: The Delaware Water Gap, separating Pennsylvania (near side) from New Jersey, provided a natural route to the western frontier. Now it's a popular camping and water recreation site.

Right and below: Independence Hall and the Liberty Bell are both located in Independence National Historical Park in Center City, Philadelphia.

Facing page: Old Main at Pennsylvania State University in the town of State College was built in 1930, replacing the original building that stood there from 1863 to 1929.

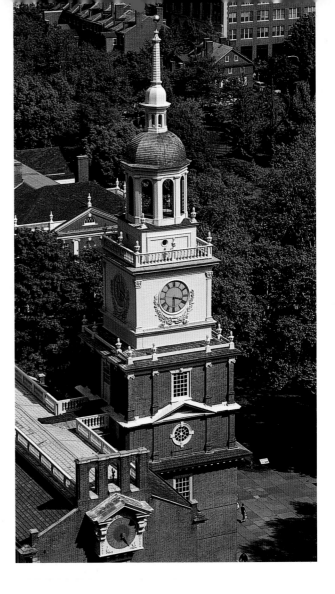

Left: In Philadelphia's Fairmount Park, Tedyuscung (d. 1738), "the last great king" of the Delaware Indians, looks over the Wissahickon Creek valley

Right: A statue of the Union army's Major General Gouverneur K. Warren rises on Little Round Top in Gettysburg National Military Park, Gettysburg. There the living General Warren stood on July 2, 1863, and ordered a bloody Union charge up the hillside when he saw that the hill was undefended and General James Longstreet's Confederates were poised to capture it.

Below: "The Thinker" by August Rodin (1840–1917) was his first bronze to be installed in a public place in France in 1906. This casting is among 124 of his sculptures in Philadelphia's Rodin Museum.

John McGrail grew up in Philadelphia and received a BA from La Salle College. John discovered his talent for photography while serving as a paratrooper in the 82nd Airborne Division. He later earned his BA in professional photography at Brooks Institute of Photography in Santa Barbara, California.

Based in New York City for many years, John traveled internationally on assignment for *Life, Time, Fortune, Discover, Sports Illustrated, National Geographic Society, Smithsonian, Scientific American,* and *US News & World Report*, among many other publications. His photographs are continually published throughout the world. The National Park Service contracted John to create panoramic murals at several parks. His photographs are used to promote travel and tourism in Arizona, South Dakota, and Newfoundland. His maritime imagery is in the permanent collection of Philadelphia's Independence Seaport Museum. John is the feature photographer for the books *Philadelphia* and *Philadelphia World Class!* and is a contributing photographer for the books *American Anthem, Manhattan, New York At Night,* and *Historic Monuments of America.* John and his family make their home in Bucks County.